EXPLORING WORLD CULTURES

Morocco

Joanne Mattern

Cavendish Square

New York

Published in 2021 by Cavendish Square Publishing, LLC
243 5th Avenue, Suite 136, New York, NY 10016

Copyright © 2021 by Cavendish Square Publishing, LLC

First Edition

Website: cavendishsq.com

This publication represents the opinions and views of the author based on his or her personal experience, knowledge, and research. The information in this book serves as a general guide only. The author and publisher have used their best efforts in preparing this book and disclaim liability rising directly or indirectly from the use and application of this book.

All websites were available and accurate when this book was sent to press.

Library of Congress Cataloging-in-Publication Data

Names: Mattern, Joanne, 1963- author.
Title: Morocco / Joanne Mattern.
Description: First edition. | New York : Cavendish Square Publishing, 2021. |
Series: Exploring world cultures | Includes index.
Identifiers: LCCN 2019049416 (print) | LCCN 2019049417 (ebook) |
ISBN 9781502656797 (library binding) | ISBN 9781502656773 (paperback) |
ISBN 9781502656780 (set) | ISBN 9781502656803 (ebook)
Subjects: LCSH: Morocco--Juvenile literature. | Morocco--History--Juvenile literature. |
Morocco--Social life and customs--Juvenile literature.
Classification: LCC DT305 .M38 2021 (print) | LCC DT305 (ebook) |
DDC 964--dc23
LC record available at https://lccn.loc.gov/2019049416
LC ebook record available at https://lccn.loc.gov/2019049417

Editor: Kristen Susienka
Copy Editor: Nathan Heidelberger
Designer: Jessica Nevins

The photographs in this book are used by permission and through the courtesy of: Cover Buzz Pictures/Alamy Stock Photo; p. 4 Mikadun/Shutterstock.com; pp. 5, 18 Ana Flasker/Shutterstock.com; p. 6 pavalena/Shutterstock.com; p. 7 Sergej Onyshko/Shutterstock.com; p. 8 akimov konstantin/Shutterstock.com; p. 9 REPORTERS ASSOCIES/Gamma-Rapho via Getty Images; p. 10 Belish/Shutterstock.com; p. 11 Bumble Dee/Shutterstock.com; p. 12 Fly_and_Dive/Shutterstock.com; p. 13 cornfield/Shutterstock.com; pp. 14, 19 LapailrKrapai/Shutterstock.com; p. 15 tenkl/Shutterstock.com; p. 16 Yavuz Sariyildiz/Shutterstock.com; p. 17 Ariya J/Shutterstock.com; p. 20 Ruslan Kalnitsky/Shutterstock.com; p. 21 Luisa Puccini/Shutterstock.com; p. 22 aaabbbccc/Shutterstock.com; p. 23 Keith Wheatley/Shutterstock.com; p. 24 Martin Silva Cosentino/Shutterstock.com; p. 25 Olena_Znak/iStock/Getty Images Plus; p. 26 cdrin/Shutterstock.com; p. 27 Jakub Zajic/Shutterstock.com; p. 28 Tatiana Bralnina/Shutterstock.com; p. 29 Matej Kastelic/Shutterstock.com.

Some of the images in this book illustrate individuals who are models. The depictions do not imply actual situations or events.

CPSIA compliance information: Batch #CS20CSQ: For further information contact Cavendish Square Publishing LLC, New York, New York, at 1-877-980-4450.

Printed in the United States of America

Find us on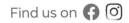

Contents

Morocco is not a large country. However, it has many different kinds of land. It has mountains, beaches, plains, and deserts. It's also a place with different **cultures** and **traditions**.

Morocco's mountains are home to ancient buildings.

More than 34 million people live in Morocco. Most of them live along the coast. Fewer people live in the mountains and desert.

Most of the people in Morocco are Arabs. That means their families came from the Middle East a long time ago. However, parts of the nation were once ruled by France and Spain. These countries **influenced** Morocco's buildings, cultures, and traditions.

The Moroccan city of Tangier glows with color at night.

Morocco's people share an interesting history. They keep ancient traditions but are also part of the modern world. Like other nations, Morocco has seen hard times and good times. Its people enjoy different foods and games. They work hard and spend time with their families and friends. Let's learn more about the land of Morocco!

Geography

Morocco is located on the northwestern corner of Africa. It covers 172,414 square miles (446,550 square kilometers). Algeria lies along Morocco's eastern

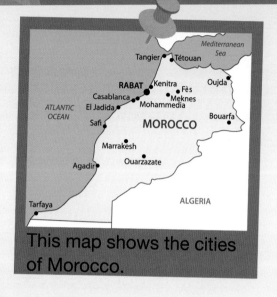

This map shows the cities of Morocco.

border. An area called Western Sahara lies to the south. Morocco claims Western Sahara as its own. However, other nations don't agree that this land is part of Morocco.

FACT!

The Strait of Gibraltar is a narrow waterway that separates Morocco from Spain, just 8 miles (13 kilometers) to the north.

Weather

Morocco's desert can be very hot in the summer and very cold in the winter. Weather on the coast is milder than in the desert.

The Atlantic Ocean lies on Morocco's western coast. The Mediterranean Sea and the Strait of Gibraltar lie to the north.

The Sahara, a desert, spreads across much of eastern

A team of camels makes its way across the Sahara.

and southern Morocco. The Atlas Mountains rise in the south and continue across the eastern border. The Rif Mountains are in the north. **Fertile** plains lie between the Rif Mountains and the Mediterranean Sea. The Moulouya River flows from the Atlas Mountains into the Mediterranean Sea and is very important to Moroccans.

History

Parts of ancient Roman cities are found in Morocco.

Groups of people traveled across North Africa about 1 million years ago. Much later, **nomads** called the Berbers came to North Africa. Ancient Romans also lived here. In 680, Arabian warriors came to the area. They became the rulers of Morocco.

From the 1500s to the 1800s, many European countries wanted to control Morocco. Morocco fought back. However, in 1912, its ruler, Sultan Abd al-Hafid, signed the **Treaty** of Fès. This treaty

The skeleton of a teenager who lived 50,000 years ago was discovered in Morocco in 1933.

Morocco has many problems with its neighbors. The native people in Western Sahara don't want to be part of Morocco. Many nations agree with them. The border between Morocco and Algeria has also been closed since 1994 because of many attacks.

gave control of Morocco to France and Spain.

Morocco remained a French colony until 1956. Then, it became an independent country led by a Moroccan ruler named Mohammed V. Since then, Morocco has grown as a modern country and faced new challenges.

King Mohammed V ruled Morocco until his death in 1961.

VOTE ✓

Morocco's government has three parts: executive, legislative, and judicial. The executive branch is led by the king and the prime minister. The prime minister oversees the laws. He or she also chooses

Morocco's prime minister speaks to the press in 2018.

cabinet ministers. They help lead different parts of the government, like health care and education.

FACT!

Morocco created its first **constitution** in 1962. The constitution has changed several times over the years. In 2011, a new constitution was written.

The red part of Morocco's flag stands for the dynasty, or family line, that rules Morocco. The star stands for Islam, the main religion in Morocco.

A soldier wears Morocco's flag on his uniform.

The legislative branch makes the laws. Members of Parliament form this branch. There are two parts of Parliament: the House of Representatives and the House of Councilors. The House of Representatives has 395 members. The House of Councilors has 120 members.

The judicial branch is made up of courts. The Supreme Court is the most important court. Morocco's system of laws is based on Islamic law and French and Spanish law.

Almost half of Moroccans work in farming. They grow fruits, vegetables, olives, and grains. Morocco's farmers use man-made waterways called canals to bring water to their

Olives are one of the most popular products grown in Morocco.

fields. Farmers also raise sheep and goats. These animals supply meat, wool, and dairy products.

Fishing is an important job in the country. Morocco sends seafood all over the world.

Mining is also an important part of Morocco's

FACT!

Morocco has one of the most successful **economies** in North Africa.

A Rich City

Casablanca is an important city in Morocco. Many banks and other businesses have offices here. The city's Morocco Mall is one of the largest malls in Africa.

economy. The country produces **minerals** like iron, copper, lead, and zinc. Morocco's workers make rugs, clothing, and shoes. Factories also make

Workers head to a mine in the Atlas Mountains.

cars, trucks, and other machines people use.

About one-third of Moroccans work in jobs that help others, like doctors, office workers, teachers, and hotel workers.

13

Morocco is home to many animals. Some examples are wild goats, camels, red foxes, desert hares, and the Barbary macaque—a type of monkey. Reptiles and birds are found here too.

Storks fly from Europe to spend the winter in Morocco's warmer weather.

Morocco's valleys and mountains support olive, eucalyptus, and oak trees. Cedar trees grow high in the mountains. Desert plants include cacti, bushes, and herbs.

FACT!

Morocco wants to get more than half of its energy from **renewable sources** by 2030.

Pollution

Pollution is a problem for Moroccans. It's very bad in big cities. Fumes from cars and trucks pollute the air. Air pollution and noise pollution hurt people and animals. Water pollution brings sicknesses. Morocco is trying to stop pollution.

Pollution is making it harder to breathe in Morocco's cities.

Much of Morocco's fuel and electricity comes from oil and gas. However, using different energy sources can save the environment, or the natural world. Morocco is trying to get more of its energy, or power, from sunlight and wind. Waterpower is becoming more common too.

The People Today

More than 34 million people live in Morocco. Most of them are Arabs or Berbers. These groups have been in Morocco for more than 1,000 years.

A Berber wearing traditional clothes walks with his camel.

Berbers belong to three different tribes: Riffians, Chleuhs, and Soussi. Most Arabs live near the coast and in the cities.

People have also come to Morocco from Europe. Many have come from Spain and

FACT!

Most Moroccans live in the western part of Morocco, away from the desert.

16

The Moors

Long ago, Berbers and Arabs married people from Spain and Portugal. These people became known as Moors. The Moors had a large influence on Morocco's art and buildings. However, they aren't seen as a separate group today.

Portugal, which are close to Morocco. Other people have come from different nations in Africa and the Middle East.

The people of Morocco are influenced by their cultural backgrounds and where they came from. They speak different languages and have different traditions.

Women and children relax outside the old city wall of Fès.

More than half of Morocco's people live in cities. Casablanca is the largest city. It's on the northwestern coast. About 3.7 million people live

Children learn the alphabet and other basic skills in school.

there. Rabat is another big city. Morocco's cities are very crowded. People walk or ride motorbikes through the narrow streets.

People in the country often live in stone or

FACT!

Most Moroccan cities are surrounded by walls. These walls were built hundreds of years ago to keep out enemies.

Medinas and Souks

Medinas are old, crowded parts of a city. They're often filled with poor people but also have many people selling items on the street. Souks are market areas. Moroccans shop at souks for fresh foods, spices, and home goods.

brick buildings. Desert homes are made of palm tree leaves packed with mud. Some Berbers are nomads and live in tents.

Shops line a narrow street in Rabat.

Children generally start school when they're seven years old. They study math, science, history, Islam, and languages. After high school, some students go to college. Others go to technical schools to learn skills like carpentry.

Religion

Almost everyone in Morocco follows the religion, or belief system, of Islam. Followers of Islam are called Muslims. Islam became Morocco's official religion in the seventh century. Muslims follow the teachings of the Prophet

Casablanca's Hassan II Mosque is the largest mosque in the nation.

Muhammad. They use these teachings in every part of life.

Muslims pray five times a day. They often go to a religious building called a mosque. Every city

FACT!

Ninety-nine percent of people who live in Morocco are Muslim.

Minarets and Muezzins

Mosques have tall, thin towers called minarets. A man called the muezzin stands in the minaret to call the faithful to pray. If they can't make it to the mosque, Muslims can pray anywhere, including at home, school, or work.

and village in Morocco has one. At the mosque, Muslims pray and listen to teachings from religious leaders called imams.

Not everyone in Morocco is Muslim. There are also small groups of Jewish and Christian people. Most Jewish people live in Rabat and Casablanca.

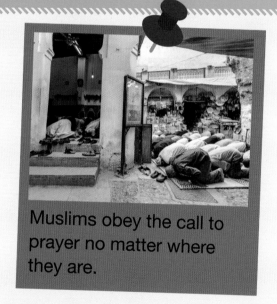

Muslims obey the call to prayer no matter where they are.

Language

Morocco has two official languages. They're Arabic and Berber. Three of the main Berber languages spoken in Morocco are Tarifit or Rifian, Tamazight, and Tachelhit.

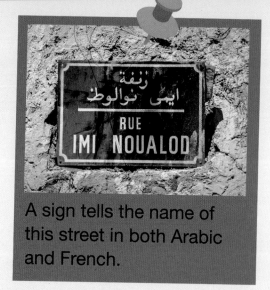

A sign tells the name of this street in both Arabic and French.

Tamazight is the official Berber language spoken in this country.

Arabic is used in school and in business in Morocco. For everyday activities, Moroccans speak an Arabic **dialect** called Darija.

Road signs are often written in both Arabic and French in Morocco.

The Arabic Language

The Arabic language uses its own alphabet. Letters read from right to left. There are no capital or lowercase letters. The Arabic alphabet has 28 consonants and 6 vowels.

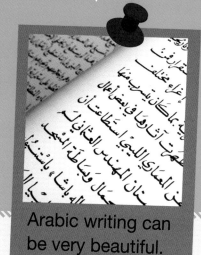

Arabic writing can be very beautiful.

The Berber languages have their own alphabet. Sometimes, though, they're written using the Arabic alphabet.

Other languages are spoken in different parts of the country. French is often used in business and in government. English is also becoming more commonly known in big cities. Children in school are learning English too.

23

Morocco is well known for its beautiful art, rugs, and other objects. Furniture is carved with silver and copper patterns.

Berber musicians perform on traditional instruments in the Sahara.

Chabbi (or *chaabi*) is the most popular music in Morocco. It mixes different styles from other countries. *Raï*, which comes from Algeria, is also popular, and so is hip-hop, which is called *hibhub* in Morocco.

FACT!

Muslims follow the Islamic calendar, which is different from the American calendar. On the American calendar, the dates of Muslim holidays change from year to year.

National Holidays

Moroccans also celebrate government holidays. Independence Day on November 18 celebrates the day Morocco won its freedom from France. July 30 is Throne Day. Parades and speeches celebrate the day King Mohammed VI came to power in 1999.

Fireworks light the sky at the end of many celebrations in Moroccan cities.

Moroccans celebrate many Muslim holidays. Muslims fast, or eat very little food, during the month of Ramadan. After Ramadan, they celebrate Eid al-Fitr, or the end of the fasting time. Another important holiday is the Prophet Muhammad's birthday.

25

Fun and Play

Soccer is the most popular sport in Morocco. Groups of young people play in streets and fields. Fans enjoy watching soccer games in the huge Mohammed V Stadium in Casablanca.

Any open place is great for a game of soccer in Morocco.

People who live along the coast of Morocco enjoy different water sports. Swimming, sailing, and surfing are popular. Skiers travel to the

People who live in the desert in Morocco enjoy camel racing. Other Moroccans like to race horses.

Every year, Morocco hosts the Marathon des Sables, or Sand Marathon. Runners race over 150 miles (240 km) of sand and rocks. It takes seven days to finish the course.

Atlas Mountains to enjoy the steep, snowy slopes. People also surf in the desert! They zoom down tall hills of sand on flat boards.

A group of young people enjoy sand surfing in the Sahara.

Moroccans like board games too. Backgammon and chess are very popular. People also enjoy spending time with family and friends as they walk through city streets or visit parks and museums.

Food

People in Morocco love to share food with family and friends. Dinner is the main meal of the day. Popular meals include meat and vegetables served with

Chicken and vegetables simmer in a tagine, creating a tasty meal.

rice or a grain-like food called couscous. Bread is eaten with every meal and is often used to scoop up food and soak up sauces. Tagine is a special Moroccan stew made of meat and vegetables. It's

FACT!

Moroccan food uses many tasty spices, such as cinnamon, cumin, ginger, and saffron.

The most popular drink in Morocco is mint tea. It's served with every meal. Moroccans also enjoy coffee with hot milk, as well as fruit juices. Fruit, milk, and ice are mixed in a popular drink called *sharbat*.

also the name of the dish in which the meal is served.

Moroccans love sweet food. They fill pastries with almonds, dates, and figs and dip

Moroccan markets are filled with a colorful and tasty selection of spices.

them in honey or sugar. Rice pudding with nuts is another popular dessert, and so are different kinds of fruit.

29

Glossary

cabinet   A group of people who help the leader of a country.

constitution   A document that sets out the rules of a nation.

culture   A country or group's beliefs, practices, or ways of life.

dialect   A version of a language spoken in just one area.

economy   The way things are made, bought, sold, and used in a country or area.

fertile   Able to grow a lot of crops.

influence   To have an effect on something.

mineral   Something that is naturally found in the earth, like gold or silver.

nomad   A person who travels from place to place.

renewable source   Something used to create electricity that doesn't run out, such as wind or sunlight.

tradition   Something done in a family or group for many years.

treaty   An official agreement made between two governments.

Find Out More

Books

Blauer, Ettagale, and Jason Lauré. *Morocco*. New York, NY: Scholastic, 2016.

Leavitt, Amie Jane. *We Visit Morocco*. Hockessin, DE: Mitchell Lane Publishers, 2012.

Strassheim, Nathalie. *Ayo's Awesome Adventures in Rabat*. Chicago, IL: World Book, Inc., 2019.

Website

National Geographic Kids: Morocco
https://kids.nationalgeographic.com/explore/countries/morocco
Learn about Morocco's history, geography, and culture at this fun website, which includes a map.

Video

Morocco Geography for Kids
https://www.youtube.com/watch?v=F3oaiRo3fdU
This cartoon video takes viewers on a tour of Morocco's different regions.

Index

About the Author

Joanne Mattern is the author of more than 250 books for children. She specializes in writing nonfiction and has explored many different places in her writing. Her favorite topics include history, travel, sports, biography, and animals. Joanne lives in New York State with her husband, four children, and several pets.